CHOCOLATE MODELING CAKE TOPPERS

101 tasty ideas for candy clay,
modeling chocolate, and other
fondant alternatives

CHOCOLATE MODELING CAKE TOPPERS

RAMLA KHAN

A QUINTET BOOK

First edition for the United States and Canada published
in 2015 by Barron's Educational Series, Inc.

All inquiries should be addressed to:
Barron's Educational Series, Inc.
250 Wireless Boulevard
Hauppauge, NY 11788
www.barronseduc.com

Library of Congress Control Number:
2014957363

ISBN: 978-1-4380-0529-4

QTT.MODC
Conceived, designed, and produced by:
Quintet Publishing Limited
4th Floor, Sheridan House
114–116 Western Road
Hove, East Sussex
BN3 1DD
UK

Designer: Bonnie Bryan
Photographer: Ian Garlick
Food Styling Assistant: Rewa Kaiwai
Art Director: Michael Charles
Editorial Director: Emma Bastow
Publisher: Mark Searle
Editorial Assistant: Ella Lines
Publishing Assistant: Alice Sambrook

Printed in China by 1010 Printing
International Limited

9 8 7 6 5 4 3 2 1

Contents

Introduction

When I was a child, life revolved around good food and decadent desserts, so I naturally developed a passion for creating glorious treats—much to the delight of my family. They would look forward to my baking experiments and encourage me to try new things, even though I would leave behind a huge mess in the kitchen!

Life then took a different turn when I decided to embark upon a career in dentistry. However, it wasn't long before the creative baker inside me was dying to showcase those skills again. I decided to set up The Enchanting Cake Company, my very own baking business, and focused on creating custom-made wedding designs.

The inspiration for many of the projects in this book comes from my experience in the wedding industry. Gone are the days of traditional white wedding cakes—modern brides and grooms want a stunning focal point that breaks from the norm. The emerging trends of modern day weddings are reflected within these pages.

As a cake designer you work with many different mediums, but modeling chocolate is one of my favorites. It provides the unique combination of exquisite taste and versatility, blends seamlessly, and is one of the only materials that can be used to cover a cake as well as create miniature toppers for it. And it tastes great.

Featuring helpful tricks and step-by-step techniques, as well as shortcuts and advice on how to achieve the perfect finish, this book will guide you through the cake decorating process. Tips for creating cake toppers for every occasion will enable even the most novice of cake decorators to turn their everyday bake into an original masterpiece.

Themed chapters feature showstopper cake toppers that you can recreate using simple techniques. Once you have mastered these skills you can develop your own unique design and experiment with different colors and customizations to make your cake really individual. Enjoy!

Ramla Khan

Working with modeling chocolate

Modeling chocolate is a versatile modeling medium that is strong and flexible, and has a very long working time. So you can leave your model on your workspace and come back to it after a break and it's still workable, unlike fondant and gumpaste. It also tastes great! It can be bought ready-made but it is really easy to make yourself, too.

Making modeling chocolate

* 1 LB 2 OZ (500 G) WHITE CHOCOLATE CHIPS
* ⅔ CUP (170 ML) CORN SYRUP

1 Melt the chocolate in a microwave oven or a double boiler until smooth and runny. Warm up the corn syrup for 30 seconds in the microwave and add it to the melted chocolate.

2 Start to mix slowly with a spatula and make sure you don't overmix, otherwise the mixture will become too oily. Once it starts to come together, blend until there are no white streaks in the mixture.

3 Pour out onto a long piece of plastic wrap and wrap it up. Leave it for a few hours or overnight, then unwrap and knead. It may have become hard at this point, so you may need to warm it slightly in the microwave. Knead it until it becomes pliable. The modeling chocolate is now ready to use.

Tips

Some problems can occur with modeling chocolate, which can be fixed quite easily if you have a little patience.

• If it becomes too oily due to overmixing when you added the corn syrup, knead it once it has set. The oil should knead back into the chocolate, but make sure you don't overheat it. Take breaks in between kneading if your hands are too warm.

• If it is dry and crumbly, you may need to add more corn syrup. Warm up 2–3 tablespoons of corn syrup and add it to the modeling chocolate. Knead the corn syrup into the chocolate until the mixture comes together and becomes smooth.

Making candy clay

Modeling chocolate has a slightly yellow tinge, as it is made using real white chocolate. If you require a purer white, try using candy melts instead of real chocolate. It will give you a very similar texture to modeling chocolate but has a bright white color, so you have the properties of modeling chocolate but the color of white fondant.

* 1 LB 2 OZ (500 G) CANDY MELTS
* ½ CUP (120 ML) CORN SYRUP

1 Melt the candy melts in a microwave oven or a double boiler until smooth and runny. Warm up the corn syrup for 30 seconds in the microwave and add it to the melted candy melts.

2 Start to mix slowly with a spatula and make sure you don't overmix, otherwise the mixture will become too oily. Once it starts to come together, blend until there are no white streaks in the mixture.

3 Pour out onto a long piece of plastic wrap and wrap it up. Leave for a few hours or overnight, then unwrap and knead. It may have become hard at this point, so you may need to warm it slightly in the microwave. Knead it until it becomes pliable. The candy clay is now ready to use.

Tips

Although white candy clay can be colored really easily using concentrated liquid or paste color (see pages 10-11), you can quickly mix up large batches of colored candy clay by using pre-colored candy melts.

Coloring modeling chocolate

If you are using a large amount of colored modeling chocolate, you can color it at the making stage (see page 8) or use colored candy melts (see page 9). When you have melted the chocolate, add a few drops of concentrated liquid or paste color to the chocolate or candy melts, then continue to add the corn syrup.

However, if you only need a small amount of each color for a project, then you can color it in the same way as you would with fondant. There are many ways to color the modeling chocolate using liquids, gels, or powdered colors. But I prefer using paste colors, as you get a very concentrated color in a tiny amount of paste.

Dab a small amount of paste color onto the tip of a toothpick (see above). Smear this onto the modeling chocolate and knead it in until you achieve a uniform color. As the paste color is very strong, add a tiny amount to start with and keep adding small amounts to build up the color.

To color a large amount of modeling chocolate, color a small ball of modeling chocolate to a darker shade than needed, then knead this into a larger ball of white modeling chocolate (see above). This method is much easier than trying to color a large amount of modeling chocolate.

To create a marbled effect, knead together 2 colors, but stop before they are mixed uniformly. When you roll out the modeling chocolate you will create a marbled effect (see below). This works very well with a combination of gray and white or brown and white to create natural stone and marble effects.

Romantic Vintage

Soft pastel shades and romantic roses make up this
pretty theme. Try experimenting with other muted
colors, such as dove gray and blush, for an elegant cake
that will be sure to wow your guests.

Roses

Ingredients

* TYLOSE POWDER
* MODELING CHOCOLATE, COLORED PINK

Tools

* ROLLING PIN
* ROSE PETAL CUTTER
* TOOTHPICK
* PALETTE KNIFE

1 Knead some tylose powder into the modeling chocolate (see page 143). Roll out some of the modeling chocolate to a thickness of 2 mm.

2 Using a rose petal-shaped cutter, cut 4–16 petals, depending on how large and full you want the rose to be. Note that the point of a petal is its base. Take 3 petal shapes for the first layer of petals. Curl the top edges by turning them over a toothpick.

3 Roll out an olive-sized piece of paste and shape it into a cone. The point of the cone will form the visible center of your rose.

4 Wrap the 3 curled petals, one at a time, around the central cone, overlapping their edges slightly. Stop after applying this first layer of petals to form a rose bud.

5 If you wish to make a larger rose, continue adding layers of petals in odd numbers—use 5 petals for the next layer, 7 for the next, and so on. Pinch around the base of the rose to secure the petals, then use a palette knife to cut off any excess.

Leaves

Ingredients

* TYLOSE POWDER
* MODELING CHOCOLATE, COLORED GREEN

Tools

* ROLLING PIN
* PLUNGER LEAF CUTTER WITH VEINS
* FOAM DRYING TRAY
* DUST COLOR IN GREEN
* REJUVENATOR SPIRIT
* PAINTBRUSH
* CONFECTIONERS' GLAZE

1 Knead some tylose powder into the modeling chocolate (see page 143). Roll out the modeling paste to a thickness of 2 mm. Using a plunger leaf cutter, cut out the leaf shapes. Before releasing each leaf, use the cutter to indent the pattern of the veins into the leaf cut out.

2 Place the leaf shapes across the ridges of a foam drying tray at different angles to give them natural shapes. Let them dry.

3 Once the leaves are dry, mix some green dust color into a little rejuvenator spirit and apply this with a paintbrush to highlight the veins on each leaf, adding depth and dimension. If you wish to give the leaves a shiny finish, paint a coating of confectioners' glaze onto each leaf and let them dry for 1 hour.

Flag Banner

1 Knead some tylose powder into the modeling chocolate (see page 143). Select 2 colors of modeling chocolate to use for the striped flag banner. Roll out each to 2 mm.

2 Using a ruler, measure and cut strips of equal widths and roughly equal lengths using a knife or a cutting wheel.

When choosing pairs of colors for the stripes and polka dots, try either striking color contrasts or dark and pale versions of similar hues

3 Lay the strips side by side in alternating colors, making sure that there are no gaps between the strips.

Ingredients

* TYLOSE POWDER
* MODELING CHOCOLATE, COLORED IN 4 COLORS OF YOUR CHOICE

Tools

* ROLLING PIN
* RULER
* KNIFE OR CUTTING WHEEL
* SMALL CIRCLE CUTTER OR PIPING TIP
* TRIANGLE CUTTER
* CAKE SMOOTHER

4 Gently roll along the strips to join them. Ensure you roll along the lengths of the strips, rather than across them, to avoid distorting the lines. Now use a triangle cutter or a scalpel and ruler to cut out triangles from the striped modeling chocolate. Set aside.

5 Roll out the remaining 2 pieces of colored modeling chocolate to a thickness of 2 mm. Use a small circle cutter or a piping tube to cut small circles from 1 color. Arrange these on the other piece of rolled out modeling chocolate in a regular polka dot pattern. Gently roll the rolling pin across the top to flatten the dots into the layer of modeling chocolate beneath. Now cut out triangles using the triangle cutter.

6 To make the banner "string," roll a ball of modeling paste into a sausage shape, then continue rolling with a cake smoother to form a long, thin cylinder. Place in a swag shape on your cake. Position the triangles along the string to resemble a banner.

Bows

1 Knead some tylose powder into the modeling chocolate (see page 143). Roll out the modeling chocolate to a thickness of 2 mm. Cut 2 strips of equal length to make the loose ends of the bow.

2 Using 1 point of a triangle cutter, or a scalpel and ruler, cut a triangle shape from one end of each strip. Run a quilting tool along the lengths of the 2 long edges on each strip, about 1 mm in from the edge, to make indents. Place one strip on top of the other at a 90-degree angle. Set aside, or place on your cupcake or cake in position.

3 Cut 2 more strips of equal width and double the length you want for each bow loop. Again, use the quilting tool to make decorative indents along the longer edges.

Tools

* ROLLING PIN
* RULER
* TRIANGLE CUTTER OR SCALPEL
* QUILTING TOOL
* PLASTIC WRAP OR TISSUE

4 Fold each strip in half to make a bow loop. Press the ends together, then pinch in the middle to make natural-looking folds. Place some scrunched up plastic wrap or tissue inside the curved part of each bow loop to give it shape. Let it dry for 24 hours.

To make polka dot and striped bows, use the methods on pages 16–17 to make patterned modeling chocolate from which to cut the bows

5 Position the bow loops on the join of the prepared ribbon ends and push down to attach. Roll out some more modeling chocolate and cut a strip that is the same width as the bow ends. Again, run the quilting tool along the two outside edges. Place this across the middle of the bow to cover the point where the loops join, and tuck it under the bow on either side.

Painted Hearts

Ingredients
* TYLOSE POWDER
* MODELING CHOCOLATE
* DUST COLORS IN PINK, RED, WHITE, AND GREEN

Tools
* ROLLING PIN
* HEART CUTTER
* PAINTBRUSH
* REJUVENATOR SPIRIT

1 Knead some tylose powder into the modeling chocolate (see page 143). Roll out some modeling chocolate to a thickness of 2–3 mm. Cut out hearts using a heart cutter. Allow to dry for 24 hours or until hard.

2 Mix some pink dust color into a little rejuvenator spirit. Using a paintbrush, paint pink rose petals onto the heart shapes at regular intervals, using a circular motion to create the petal shapes.

3 Darken the pink mixture by adding red dust color and use to add definition to the roses. Mix white dust color into a little rejuvenator spirit and use to paint curved lines along the petal edges.

4 Mix some green dust color into some rejuvenator spirit. Use this to paint green leaves at the base of each rose to finish.

Windmills

Ingredients

* TYLOSE POWDER
* MODELING CHOCOLATE

Tools

* ROLLING PIN
* RULER
* SCALPEL
* TOOTHPICK

1 Knead some tylose powder into the modeling chocolate (see page 143). Roll out modeling chocolate to a thickness of 3 mm. Measure and cut out a square using a ruler and scalpel. Mark the middle point of the square with a toothpick.

2 Cut a diagonal line running from each corner of the square to the middle, stopping 5 mm away from the marked point at the middle of the square. The lines mark out 4 equal triangles. Take the left-hand point of triangle and bring it to the middle point of the square.

3 Take the left-hand point of each of the remaining 3 triangles and bring them, one by one, to the middle point. Place a pearl over the join in the middle.

Steampunk

Step back in time to the Victorian days, when science
and fantasy collided, to create a cake featuring metallic
cogs and wheels, and an old-fashioned pocket watch.
Reimagine the past with your own interpretation of
how the world could have been back then.

Cogs & Wheels

1 To make the cogs, roll a ball of modeling chocolate and place into a cog mold.

2 Roll the rolling pin over the top of the mold to flatten the modeling chocolate completely. Remove any excess modeling chocolate with a knife. Place the mold in the freezer for 10 minutes.

3 Remove the chocolate from the mold and let it dry for 24 hours. Apply some bronze or gold edible paint with a paintbrush to give the cog a metallic look.

Tip

If you don't have a cog-shaped mold, roll out some modeling chocolate to a thickness of 2 mm. Cut out a large circle using a pastry cutter. Using a small square cutter, cut out small indents along the edge of the circle.

4 To make the wheels, roll out balls of modeling chocolate and use an assortment of cutters and piping tips to make wheel and cog designs within the circle and to shape the outside. Remember that you can use the cutters to make indents rather than full cuts, too.

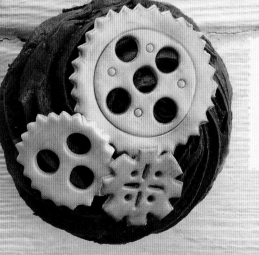

You can insert wire into the sides of the cogs and wheels, then suspend these over the cake so that the shapes appear to float above it

5 Allow the wheels to dry fully, then apply a coating of metallic edible paint to finish.

Pocket Watch

Use luster dust in a darker gold or bronze shade to darken the edges of the pocket watch for a more antique effect

1 Knead some tylose powder into some of the white and gold modeling chocolate (see page 143). Roll out this gold modeling chocolate mixed with tylose powder to a thickness of ¼ in (5 mm). Cut out a circle using the larger circle cutter and set aside. Roll out white modeling chocolate mixed with tylose powder to a thickness of 3 mm. Use the smaller circle cutter to cut out a circle.

2 Place the smaller white circle on top of the gold circle in the center. Now roll a long thin sausage shape using gold modeling chocolate, or use the sugar gun to shape it. Wrap the sausage around the white clock face to give the clock face a gold rim. Use your finger to blend the join together.

3 To make the watch crown, roll a small ball of gold modeling chocolate and flatten slightly. Use a toothpick to make indents at regular intervals along the outside. Roll another small ball of gold chocolate, pinch using your finger and thumb to create a cone shape. Roll a thin sausage shape and bend twice to make the handle of the crown.

4 Roll out long thin sausages of gold modeling chocolate and cut them into 1¼-in (3-cm) lengths.

5 Bend each length into a loop. Thread one loop through another and pinch the opening closed. Repeat with the remaining loops to make a long watch chain.

6 Use edible glue (see page 142) to attach the parts of the winder to the rim of the pocket watch, using the picture as a placement guide. Let it dry. Paint with metallic edible paint. Write on the clock numbers using black edible pen.

Ingredients

* TYLOSE POWDER
* MODELING CHOCOLATE COLORED GOLD AND WHITE
* EDIBLE GLUE
* GOLD OR BRONZE METALLIC EDIBLE PAINT
* EDIBLE BLACK PEN

Tools

* ROLLING PIN
* CIRCLE CUTTERS IN 2 SIZES
* SUGAR GUN (OPTIONAL)
* TOOTHPICK
* PAINTBRUSH

Buttons

Ingredients

* TYLOSE POWDER
* MODELING CHOCOLATE
* GOLD OR BRONZE
  METALLIC LUSTER DUST
  OR METALLIC EDIBLE
  PAINT

Tools

* ROLLING PIN
* CIRCLE CUTTERS IN
  2 SIZES
* TOOTHPICK
* DUSTING BRUSH

Change the colors of the buttons to vary the theme. Pastel shades are perfect for a cake for a baby, or use bold, bright colors for a sewing enthusiast!

1 Knead some tylose powder into the modeling chocolate (see page 143). Roll out the modeling chocolate to a thickness of 3 mm. Cut out circles using the larger circle cutter. Now use the smaller cutter to indent a circle shape around the edge of the larger circle to indicate a rim at the button's edge.

2 Use a toothpick to make either 2 or 4 button holes. Leave them to dry. Once dry, dust with metallic luster dust or paint with metallic edible paint.

Baroque Scrolls

Ingredients

* MODELING CHOCOLATE
* GOLD LUSTER DUST

Tools

* BAROQUE SCROLLS MOLD
* KNIFE
* DUSTING BRUSH

1 Roll some modeling chocolate into a ball and press it into the scroll mold. Push down firmly to fill out the entire mold. Trim off any excess modeling chocolate with a knife.

2 Place the filled mold in the freezer for 10 minutes. Remove the chocolate from the mold and let it set.

3 Using a dusting brush, dust the scroll shapes with luster dust.

Place the scrolls along the edges of your cake for a decorative border, or arrange them in pairs as cupcake toppers

Under the Sea

Delve into the depths of the ocean to discover a world of colorful sea creatures and pretty coral. Create movement and experiment with bright colors for this magical theme.

Shells & Pearls

1 Roll a little modeling chocolate into a ball and push it into one of the shapes in your shell mold. Repeat to fill the mold. Remove excess chocolate with a knife, taking care not to move the chocolate in the mold so you don't distort the shape.

2 Freeze for approximately 10 minutes so the molded chocolate retains its shape when removed from the mold. Remove from mold and let them dry.

3 Using edible paint in the color of your choice, paint the shells. Leave them to dry, then use a darker shade of edible paint to add some shadows in the recesses across the surfaces of the shells to make them look realistic.

Ingredients

* MODELING CHOCOLATE
* EDIBLE PAINTS
* LUSTER DUST

Tools

* SHELL MOLD
* KNIFE
* PAINTBRUSH
* ROLLING PIN
* SMALL CIRCLE CUTTER
* DUSTING BRUSH

4 Now make the pearls. Roll out some modeling chocolate to a thickness of ¼ in (5 mm). Cut out little circles using a circle cutter. Roll the circles into balls. Set aside to dry.

5 Finish the pearls with a dusting of luster dust to give a pearlescent finish.

Sprinkle a little brown sugar at the base of a cake, then place a number of shells and pearls on the sugar so they appear to be sitting on a bed of sand

Starfish

Ingredients
* MODELING CHOCOLATE

Tools
* ROLLING PIN
* STAR CUTTER
* SMALL ROUND PIPING TIP

1 Roll out the modeling chocolate to a thickness of ½–¾ in (1–2 cm).

2 Cut out a star shape using your star-shaped cutter. Gently twist each point to make it longer and thinner and resemble starfish "legs," then curl and twist the legs in different directions to give a realistic look.

3 Pinch the middle of the starfish up into a ridge.

Give your starfish a dusting of edible dust color to create a colorful finish, if you like. Use pictures of starfish to inspire your color choices

4 Using a piping tip with a very small circular hole, make tiny indentations all over the starfish. Alternatively, roll up tiny balls of modeling chocolate and stick these over the body and legs to achieve the same effect. Vary the sizes of the balls, and flatten them slightly once they are in place so that there are no gaps between the balls, for a realistic effect.

Coral

Ingredients

* MODELING CHOCOLATE, IN VARIOUS COLORS

Tools

* ROLLING PIN
* SCALPEL
* ASSORTMENT OF ROUND CUTTERS IN VARIOUS SIZES
* SMALL ROUND PIPING TIP
* FOAM DRYING TRAY
* SMALL BALL TOOL

1 Roll a piece of modeling chocolate into a ball, then roll out the ball to an oval shape with a thickness of 1 mm.

2 Using a scalpel, cut the edge of the rolled out modeling chocolate to give it a long, irregular rectangular shape.

3 Use the round cutters and piping tip to cut holes into the shape. Overlap the holes, and make the cuts overlap the edges of the shape to give it the natural water-worn look of a piece of coral.

4 Place the shape across the ridges of a foam drying tray to create some movement within it. Let it dry for 24 hours or until completely set.

Pastel shades work well for coral, as well as bright, electric hues—some corals look almost unnatural and even alien!

Coral weed

1 Roll a piece of modeling chocolate into a large ball. Now roll one end of the ball into a cone shape.

You could use marbled modeling chocolate, made by mixing two shades of the same color (see page 11) to give the coral a pretty pattern

2 Using a scalpel, make small cuts into the sides of the cone, but do not allow the cuts to extend right to the middle of the cone. Using your fingers, gently twist and tease the cut sections, one by one, into long spirals and undulating shapes, allowing them to overlap and curl around one another to give the impression of fronds of coral weed waving in water.

Coral rock

1 Roll a small piece of modeling chocolate into a sausage shape.

2 Insert a ball tool into one end of the sausage to create an irregular hole and expand that end of the shape.

3 Repeat steps 1 and 2 to create multiple sausage shapes. Place the shapes together side by side, with the holes pointed upward, to resemble a mass of pitted coral rock. Squeeze them together at the base to join them, then trim away any excess modeling chocolate at the base.

Combining different types of coral-shaped decorations creates a pretty and realistic effect

Water Lily

1 Roll out some white modeling chocolate to a thickness of 2 mm. Cut out 2 flowers using the largest daisy cutter. Place the flower on a foam pad, then place the rounded sphere of a ball tool on the tip of the petal and gently drag it to the center of the flower so that the petal curls up. Repeat with the remaining petals, then repeat the entire process with the remaining flower. Position one daisy on top of the other so that their petals are offset rather than aligned.

2 Cut another white daisy shape using the medium-sized daisy cutter. Curl the petal tips as described in step 1. Position this flower on top of the other daisies, again, so that their petals are offset rather than aligned. Set aside.

3 Roll a small ball of yellow modeling chocolate. Roll out the remaining yellow modeling chocolate to a thickness of 1–2 mm and cut out 2 flowers using the smallest daisy cutter. Wrap 1 of these flowers around the yellow ball, enclosing the ball completely. Curl the petal tips of the second daisy as described in step 1. Position this underneath the yellow ball, wrapping it around the ball but not enclosing it completely.

4 Place the wrapped ball on top of the white flowers in the center of the stack. If the petals are not holding their curled shapes, insert some scrunched up tissue or plastic wrap between them to help them retain their shapes. Let them dry.

* MODELING CHOCOLATE,
  COLORED WHITE,
  YELLOW, AND GREEN
* EDIBLE GLUE

Tools

* ROLLING PIN
* DAISY CUTTERS IN
  3 SIZES
* FOAM PAD
* BALL TOOL
* TISSUE PAPER OR
  PLASTIC WRAP
* LARGE ROUND CUTTER
* SCALPEL
* VEINING TOOL

Mix a little blue food coloring into some piping gel and use this to create a wavy water effect on your cupcakes or cakes as a base for your underwater-themed toppers

5 Roll out some green modeling chocolate to a thickness of 1–2 mm. Cut out a large circle using a large round cutter. Using a scalpel, cut out a thin triangle shape, with 1 point of the triangle extending from the midpoint of the circle to the edge. Use the veining tool to give the lily pad some texture. Start with the point of the tool at the center point and roll the veining tool out to the edge, working around the lily pad. Place pieces of scrunched-up tissue paper or plastic wrap under the edge of the lily pad at various points to give its shape some movement. Allow it to dry.

6 Once all the elements are dry, position the lily flower on the center of the lily pad and secure it with edible glue (see page 142).

Winter Wonderland

Take a walk through this snowy forest to make your own magical wintery scene. Adorned with snowy berries and falling twinkling snowflakes, this is the perfect theme for a winter wedding or a festive cake.

Snowballs

Ingredients

* MODELING CHOCOLATE, COLORED WHITE
* UNSWEETENED DESICCATED COCONUT

Tools

* ROLLING PIN
* CIRCLE CUTTERS IN VARIOUS SIZES

1 Roll out some white modeling chocolate to a thickness of ¾ in (2 cm). Cut out a few circles using a variety of circle cutters.

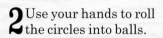

2 Use your hands to roll the circles into balls.

3 Place the balls in a bowl of desiccated coconut. Tilt the bowl to roll the balls around in order to fully coat them with the coconut flakes. Allow them to dry.

Roll the snowballs in edible white glitter instead of desiccated coconut for a glittery variation

Snowmen

1 Roll out some white modeling chocolate to a thickness of ¾ in (2 cm). Cut out a large and a small circle using the circle cutters. Use your hands to roll the circles into balls. Pierce a toothpick right through the center of the large ball so that roughly ½ in (1 cm) of it pokes out through the other side of the ball.

2 Push the small ball down onto the part of the toothpick that pokes out through the top of the large ball. Let it dry.

3 Roll a small piece of orange modeling chocolate between your fingertips to make a carrot shape for the nose. Roll 2 small balls of black modeling chocolate for the snowman's eyes, and 3 more for his buttons. Let them dry.

4 Roll some brown modeling chocolate into a ball, then shape into a thin sausage. Cut this into 3 sections—1 long and 2 short pieces. Using the picture as a guide, create a stick arm, blending the joins with your fingers. Repeat to make a second arm. Allow them to dry.

5 Roll out some black modeling chocolate to a thickness of 1 mm. Use the small round cutter to cut out a circle. Place the circle on a foam pad and use a ball tool to soften and bend its edge to give the impression of a battered hat rim.

6 Roll a piece of black modeling chocolate into a ball, then squeeze the ball in the center to shape it into a cylinder. Use your finger and thumb to pinch the bottom and top edges to flatten and give the shape of a top hat. Using edible glue (see page 142), stick the cylinder to the center of the circle to complete the hat. Let it dry.

7 Use some edible glue to attach the nose, eyes, and buttons to the snowman's head and body, using the picture here as a placement guide. Use a toothpick to pierce a hole in the body on either side in which to insert the arms, then insert them. Use edible glue to attach the hat to the top of the snowman's head. Allow the edible glue to dry before using this decoration.

To give the snowman a striped scarf, follow the instructions on pages 16–17 to make a striped length of modeling chocolate, then cut out a thin length for a scarf to wrap around the snowman's neck

Snowflakes

Ingredients

* MODELING CHOCOLATE, COLORED WHITE

Tools

* ROLLING PIN
* SNOWFLAKE PLUNGER CUTTERS IN A VARIETY OF SIZES
* LARGE SNOWFLAKE COOKIE CUTTER
* SCALPEL
* SMALL CUTTERS IN A VARIETY OF SHAPES, SUCH AS STARS AND TRIANGLES
* SMALL ROUND PIPING TIPS
* DECORATIVE PAPER PUNCH

Snowflake cutters come in a variety of shapes and sizes—select your favorite shapes and create a range of designs based on these

1 Roll out some modeling chocolate to a thickness of 2 mm. Using the finer snowflake cutters, cut out the number of snowflakes you need. Let them dry on a flat surface.

1 Roll out some modeling chocolate to a thickness of 2 mm. Use a large star or snowflake outline cutter to cut a star shape with multi-angled points. If your cutter doesn't have multi-angled points, add these using a scalpel.

No two snowflakes are the same, so let your imagination loose and vary the design of each snowflake using a range of tools

2 Using an assortment of shaped cutters, cut out shapes in the center of each snowflake to create attractive snowflake designs. Leave them to dry on a flat surface.

1 Roll out some modeling chocolate to a thickness of 1 mm. Insert the chocolate into your paper punch and push down to create pattern. Move the chocolate to expose an unpunched area to the punching plate and press down to repeat the pattern.

Paper punches come in many beautiful patterns, and can be used to make some wonderfully intricate snowflake designs

2 Remove the chocolate from the punch. Position the large outline cutter to make the best of the punched pattern and cut out a snowflake shape. Leave it to dry on a flat surface.

Try inserting floral wire into the snowflakes and suspending them over your cake to give the impression of falling snowflakes

Pine Cones

Ingredients

* MODELING CHOCOLATE, COLORED BROWN
* POWDERED SUGAR

Tools

* ROLLING PIN
* SMALL PETAL CUTTER
* FOAM DRYING PAD
* BALL TOOL

1 Roll out some modeling chocolate to a thickness of ¼ in (5 mm). Cut out many petal shapes using the small petal cutter.

Use this technique with green modeling chocolate to make a Christmas tree and attach a star shape at the top to complete

2 To shape a pine cone scale, place a petal shape on a foam pad and shape with a ball tool (see step 1, page 40). Draw out the ball tool and pinch the pointed end of the petal shape closed. Repeat with all the petal shapes.

3 Roll a piece of modeling chocolate into a large cone shape to the height that you want your pine cone to be.

4 Attach one pine cone scale to the bottom of the cone shape by the pointed, pinched end. Using the sphere of the ball tool, blend the join. Attach another scale adjacent to this one, then work around the cone to complete the first layer of scales. Position the first scale of the next layer between 2 of the scales on the first layer, and continue as before to complete the second layer. Continue in this way until the scales reach the top of the cone. Let it dry.

5 Dust the dry pine cone decoration with powdered sugar to give a wintry look.

Winter Berries

Red berries

1 Roll out small balls of red modeling chocolate. Make them of different sizes to give them a natural look.

Use these berries alone, or tie the wires together to create a bunch of berries. Make them without wires if you are using them to decorate cupcakes

2 Pierce one berry with a piece of wire and pass it through the berry. Stop when the wire is just poking through the other side. Repeat with the remaining berries and pieces of wire. Let them dry.

Tools

* 24 GAUGE FLORAL WIRE, CUT INTO 4-IN (10-CM) LENGTHS
* FLORAL FOAM
* TOOTHPICK
* PAINTBRUSH

3 Dip each berry in a little confectioners' glaze, then pierce the free end of the wire in a piece of floral foam and leave them to dry.

Gray berries

1 Roll a medium-sized ball of gray modeling chocolate. Insert a length of wire into it, but stop before it pokes through on the opposite side of the ball.

2 Use a toothpick to make tiny indents all over the surface. Leave it to dry.

Snowy Blackberries

1 Roll out a medium-sized ball of black modeling chocolate.

2 Insert a length of wire into it, but stop before it pokes through on the opposite side of the ball. Let it dry.

Instead of using semolina to cover this snowy ball, try using colored sugar or edible glitter

3 Place one tablespoon of semolina in a small bowl. Paint some confectioners' glaze over a ball. Now insert the ball into the semolina, making sure it is fully coated, then shake off any excess semolina. Let it dry.

Snowdrop

1 Roll a small piece of modeling chocolate into a ball. Insert the tip of the wire into the ball and mold the chocolate around the wire to secure it. Let it dry.

2 Roll out some white modeling chocolate to a thickness of 2 mm. Cut out a blossom shape using the blossom cutter.

3 Using a foam pad and ball tool, thin the edges of the petals (see step 1, page 40).

4 Insert the free end of the wire through the center of the blossom and pass the flower up the wire to meet the ball at the other end. Pinch the flower around the middle to join it to the ball. Leave it to dry. Once set, mix some green paste with rejuvenator spirit and paint a green outline on the outside edges of the petals.

Ingredients

* MODELING CHOCOLATE, COLORED WHITE
* GREEN PASTE COLOR

Tools

* 24 GAUGE FLORAL WIRE
* ROLLING PIN
* BLOSSOM CUTTER
* FOAM PAD
* BALL TOOL
* FREESIA CUTTER
* PAINTBRUSH
* REJUVENATOR SPIRIT

5 Roll out some white modeling chocolate to a thickness of 2 mm. Cut out the next layer of petals using a freesia cutter. Use the ball tool to thin the edges of the petals as before.

6 Insert the free end of the wire through the center of the freesia and pass the flower up the wire to meet the blossom at the other end. Pinch around the base to join them together. Bend the wire and hang the flower upside down to dry.

Wrap some green floral tape around the wires, then bend the stems over to mimic the curved shape of snowdrops

The Secret Garden

"And the secret garden bloomed and bloomed and every morning revealed new miracles," so Frances Hodgson Burnett wrote in *The Secret Garden*. Take inspiration from the classic novel and unlock your own hidden world filled with an abundance of colorful flowers and even a secret flower fairy.

Petunia

1 Roll out some modeling chocolate to thickness of 1–2 mm. Cut out a flower shape using a petunia cutter.

2 Position the petunia shape in the veiner mold (you may need to dust the mold with cornstarch first if the mold or modeling chocolate is sticky). Push down gently on the veiner mold, then remove the petunia shape from the mold and place it over the ridges of a foam drying tray to give the flower a realistic shape. Leave it to dry.

Following step 4, prepare a bundle of wires with flower centers attached, saving you time when making many of the flowers shown in this chapter

Ingredients

- ❋ MODELING CHOCOLATE, COLORED PALE PINK AND WHITE
- ❋ DEEP PINK PASTE COLOR
- ❋ EDIBLE GLUE

Tools

- ❋ ROLLING PIN
- ❋ PETUNIA CUTTER AND VEINER MOLD SET
- ❋ FOAM DRYING TRAY
- ❋ REJUVENATOR SPIRIT
- ❋ PAINTBRUSH
- ❋ 24 GAUGE FLORAL WIRE, CUT TO 4 IN (10 CM) IN LENGTH
- ❋ FLORAL FOAM BLOCK

3 Paint the inside of the center of the flower with the deep pink paste color mixed with rejuvenator spirit.

4 Roll some white modeling chocolate into a small ball. Dip the end of a length of wire into some edible glue (see page 142), then pierce the dipped end into the ball. Now pierce the loose end of the wire through the center of the inside of the flower and pull it through to bring the flower up to the ball. Pinch the base of the flower to secure it to the ball. Pierce the loose end of the wire into some floral foam and leave the flower to dry.

Blossom

1 Roll out some modeling chocolate to a thickness of 1–2 mm. Cut 2 flower shapes—1 large and 1 small—using blossom cutters.

2 Place each blossom, in turn, into the blossom veiner (you may need to dust with cornstarch if the veiner or modeling chocolate is sticky). Push down on the blossom veiner, then remove the modeling chocolate from veiner. Place the veined flowers across the ridges of a foam drying tray to shape them. Leave them to dry.

Ingredients

* MODELING CHOCOLATE, COLORED WHITE
* PINK AND GREEN OR YELLOW PETAL DUST
* EDIBLE GLUE

Tools

* ROLLING PIN
* BLOSSOM CUTTERS IN 2 SIZES
* BLOSSOM VEINER MOLD
* FOAM DRYING TRAY
* DUSTING BRUSHES
* PAINTBRUSH

3 Color the edges of both petals with some pink petal dust. Now dust the center of the smaller blossom with green or yellow petal dust.

4 Use edible glue (see page 142) to attach the smaller blossom to the center of the larger flower, positioning so that the petals of each flower are offset. Leave it to dry.

These blossoms make ideal filler flowers, as they are the perfect size for closing gaps between larger flowers, such as roses or peonies

Open Peony

1 Roll out some modeling chocolate to a thickness of 2 mm. Cut out 3 small and 6 large peony petals.

You may like to dust the edges of the peony petals with deep pink petal dust before assembling the flower, to give them some realistic shading

2 Position each peony petal, in turn, on a peony veiner. Press down gently with your hand, or roll over the shape lightly with a rolling pin, to indent the texture of the veins onto the modeling chocolate. Place the veined petals into the recesses of an apple tray to give them natural-looking curved shapes. Leave them to dry.

Ingredients

* MODELING CHOCOLATE, COLORED PALE PINK
* EDIBLE GLUE

Tools

* ROLLING PIN
* PEONY CUTTERS IN 2 SIZES
* PEONY VEINER
* MOLDED APPLE TRAY
* FLOWER FORMER
* PEARL STAMENS

3 Use a flower former to assemble the curved petal shapes into a flower. First, place 3 large petals in the former, overlapping them as shown in the picture above. Now position the remaining 3 large petals over the first layer, once again overlapping the petals, and positioning them to offset the petals of the first layer.

4 Position the 3 small petals to complete the peony. To make the flower center, roll a small ball with some modeling chocolate and attach it to the center of the flower with edible glue. Insert the pearl stamens into the ball to complete the flower. Leave to dry.

Calla Lily

1 Roll out some modeling chocolate to a thickness of 1 mm. Use a calla lily cutter to cut out a petal shape.

Make a two-tone calla lily by dusting the central area of the inside of the petal with green or yellow dust color

2 Place the petal shape on a calla lily veiner and align. Press down gently with your hand or roll a rolling pin lightly over the surface of the modeling chocolate so that the texture on the veiner is impressed upon the chocolate. Set aside.

Ingredients

* MODELING CHOCOLATE,
  COLORED WHITE
* EDIBLE GLUE
* SEMOLINA

Tools

* ROLLING PIN
* CALLA LILY PETAL
  CUTTER AND VEINER
  SET
* GREEN FLORAL TAPE
* 22 GAUGE FLORAL
  WIRE, CUT TO 4 IN
  (10 CM) IN LENGTH
* PAINTBRUSH
* FLORAL FOAM BLOCK

3 Now make the stamen. Wrap some green floral tape around the length of floral wire to make a stem. Roll some modeling chocolate into a ball with a 1¼ in (3 cm) diameter. Now roll this out into a stamen shape. Insert the stem into the stamen shape at one end and push it in without allowing it to poke through the other end. Now coat the stamen-shaped modeling chocolate with edible glue (see page 142), then dip it into a bowl of semolina.

4 Holding the stem, position the stamen in the middle of the petal. Fold one side at the base of the petal over the stem and secure with edible glue. Now fold over the other side and use glue to secure the petal. Pinch at base of the flower to secure the petals around the stamen. Pierce the loose end of the stem into floral foam and leave it to dry.

Dahlia

1 Roll out orange modeling chocolate to a thickness of 1–2 mm. Cut out 16 rose petals using a small petal cutter.

Add one or two more layers of petals if you would like the dahlia decoration to be very full

2 Use a ball tool to give each petal a cupped shape.

3 Pinch the pointed end of each petal to half-close the cup shape.

Ingredients

* MODELING CHOCOLATE, COLORED ORANGE AND YELLOW
* EDIBLE GLUE

Tools

* ROLLING PIN
* SMALL PETAL CUTTER
* BALL TOOL
* FOAM DRYING PAD
* PAINTBRUSH
* SMALL ROUND PIPING TIP

4 Roll a small ball of orange modeling chocolate and flatten to form a base for the petals. Arrange 10 petals on the base in a circle to form the first layer, attaching them to the base with some edible glue (see page 142).

5 Roll a little yellow modeling chocolate into a ball. Use a small round piping tip to make indents of little circles across the surface of the ball.

6 Arrange another 6 petals in a circle on top of the first layer of petals. Again, use edible glue to attach them together in the center of the circle. Now attach the yellow ball to the middle of the dahlia with edible glue to finish.

Fairy

1 Take a medium-sized ball of pale green modeling chocolate and roll it into a sausage shape. Roll it in the middle between your finger and thumb to create the fairy's waist.

2 Take a small piece of flesh-colored modeling chocolate and roll it into a sausage shape. Using your fingertips, pinch the middle of the shape to create the fairy's neck.

3 Split a medium-sized ball of flesh-colored modeling chocolate into 2 equal portions. Roll each of these into a long, thin sausage shape, then taper one end to make it thinner than the other.

4 Press the tapered end of each hand slightly to flatten it into the shape of a hand. Indent lines into the back of each hand with a toothpick to suggest fingers.

Ingredients

* MODELING CHOCOLATE, COLORED PALE GREEN, FLESH-COLORED, AND BROWN
* EDIBLE BLACK PAINT
* PALE PINK PETAL DUST
* EDIBLE GLUE

Tools

* ROLLING PIN
* LARGE BLOSSOM CUTTER
* FOAM DRYING PAD
* BALL TOOL
* TOOTHPICK
* PAINTBRUSHES
* DUSTING BRUSH
* MEDIUM-SIZED CIRCLE CUTTER
* CUTTING WHEEL
* SMALL PETAL CUTTER

5 Make the legs in the same way as the arms, starting with a larger piece of modeling chocolate. Bend each leg in half to make the knee.

6 Bend the leg approximately ½ in (1 cm) from the end to make the ankle, then flatten the end to make a foot.

7 Roll out some green modeling chocolate to a thickness of 2 mm. Cut out a large blossom flower shape, then place this on a foam pad and use a ball tool to soften the edges of the petals.

8 Roll some flesh-colored modeling chocolate into a medium-sized ball for the fairy's head. Pierce a toothpick through the bottom of the head, then hold the head by the stick while you draw on eyes with black edible paint. Use some pink petal dust to suggest her cheeks.

9 Make the fairy's hair. Roll out some brown modeling chocolate to a thickness of 2 mm. Cut out a circle that's just larger than the fairy's head using a medium-sized circle cutter. Use the cutting wheel to indent a pattern of lines running from the center of the circle to the edges to suggest hair.

10 Roll a small ball of brown modeling chocolate and flatten one side. Run the cutting wheel over the domed side to suggest hair in a bun.

11 Now cut out a small petal shape and make lines across the surface with the cutting wheel.

12 Begin to assemble the pieces of the fairy, starting with the body. Attach the neck to the body using edible glue.

13 Position the fairy's legs together and place them on the cake or cupcake in position.

To make this fairy completely edible, use a piece of raw spaghetti in place of the toothpick

14 Use edible glue to attach the center of the blossom shape to the top of her legs to make a skirt. Now attach the body to the center of the skirt. Secure the head by threading the toothpick through the body. Use edible glue to attach an arm to each side of the body, positioning the hands to rest on her lap. To assemble the hair, place the circle on the top of her head and gently shape it around the sphere. Glue the bun to the top of her head, then position the petal shape across her forehead as bangs.

Door

Ingredients

* MODELING CHOCOLATE, COLORED DARK BROWN
* EDIBLE GLUE

Tools

* ROLLING PIN
* WOOD GRAIN TEXTURE MAT
* CUTTING WHEEL
* PAINTBRUSH

1 Roll out some modeling chocolate to a thickness of 2 mm. Place the strip on a wood grain texture mat and, using gentle pressure, roll over it with a rolling pin so that the textured surface of the mat is indented on the side of the modeling chocolate that is exposed to the mat. If you don't have a wood grain texture mat, run a cutting wheel back and forth across the surface of the modeling chocolate to mimic the texture of wood.

2 Make a template for the door to the required size, using the picture here as a guide. Remove the textured modeling chocolate from the mat and, using your template, cut out the door shape using the cutting wheel.

3 Use a cutting wheel to cut down the center of the door. Roll 2 small pieces of modeling chocolate into balls for door handles. Finish by attaching one ball to each side of the door with edible glue.

Key

Ingredients

* MODELING CHOCOLATE, COLORED WHITE
* GOLD OR SILVER METALLIC PAINT

Tools

* KEY MOLD
* KNIFE
* SMALL PAINTBRUSH

1 Roll some modeling chocolate into a sausage shape. Insert the sausage into a key mold, then trim away any excess modeling chocolate with a knife. Freeze for 15 minutes.

2 Remove the modeling chocolate from the mold and leave to dry. Finish by painting the key with metallic paint.

Cut the key in half through the shaft, then stick it to the door shown opposite in place of a door handle so it appears as if a key is in a lock

Urn

1 Roll out some modeling chocolate to a thickness of 2 mm. Cut out a circle using a circle cutter with a diameter of 1½ in (4 cm). Now cut out 2 squares—one measuring 1½ x 1½ in (4 x 4 cm), the other 1¾ x 1¾ in (4.5 x 4.5 cm).

2 Now stack the pieces into an urn base, starting with the large square at the bottom, followed by the smaller square, with the circle on top, sticking the layers together with edible glue (see page 142).

3 Use the smile tool to make a pattern of indents around the edge of the circle at the top of the stack. Roll some modeling chocolate into a thick sausage that's roughly 2 in (5 cm) long. Pinch one end in to taper it—this will be the top of the stand. Pinch out the edges of the other end to flatten it into a circular base with a diameter of 1½ in (4 cm). Position the stand on the base, align the base with the circle on the top of the stack and attach using edible glue.

4 Insert a toothpick through the center of the top of the urn stand so that roughly ¼ in (5 mm) extends up from the top of the stand. Leave it to dry. Roll out some modeling chocolate and cut a small circle with a diameter of ½ in (1 cm). Use the smile tool to make a pattern of indents around the edge of the circle. Position this circle with the pattern facing downward over the urn stand and pierce the tip of the toothpick through the circle's center.

Ingredients

* MODELING CHOCOLATE, COLORED MARBLED GRAY
* EDIBLE GLUE

Tools

* ROLLING PIN
* PAINTBRUSH
* 1½ IN (4 CM) AND 3¼ IN (8 CM) CIRCLE CUTTERS
* 1½ IN (4 CM) AND 1¾ IN (4.5 CM) SQUARE CUTTERS
* SMILE TOOL
* TOOTHPICK
* HALF FOAM BALL

5 Roll out more modeling chocolate to a thickness of 3 mm. Cut out a large circle and shape the circle into a bowl shape on a foam ball half. Let dry for at least a couple of hours.

6 Roll 25 small balls of modeling chocolate into tapered cones. Attach these to the outside of the bowl using edible glue, ensuring the tips overlap the rim of the bowl by ¼ in (5 mm).

7 Once dry, paint the top surface of the ½ in (1 cm) circle positioned at the top of the urn stand with edible glue. Place the upturned urn bowl over this and press down to pierce through it with the tip of the toothpick. Attach a small blob of modeling chocolate to the inside of the urn bowl to cover the tip of the toothpick poking through. Let it dry.

Oriental

Travel to the Far East with this oriental-inspired theme. From delicate cherry blossoms to a miniature tea set, you'll be able to create a variety of toppers with which to honor your guests.

Cherry Blossom

Roll out long, thin sausage shapes using brown modeling chocolate, then place these on your cake to resemble branches and attach cherry blossom stems to them

1 Roll out some pink modeling chocolate to a thickness of 1 mm. Using a blossom cutter and veiner set, cut out a blossom shape and give it veins (see step 2, page 62).

2 Use nose pliers to bend a hook at the end of the length of floral wire. Bundle together 2–3 cake-decorating stamens, then hook the wire around middle of their lengths. Use the pliers to press the hook closed around the stamens to hold the stamens in place.

3 Roll out some dark pink modeling chocolate. Use a calyx cutter to cut out a small size calyx shape.

Ingredients

* MODELING CHOCOLATE, COLORED PALE PINK AND DARK PINK
* EDIBLE GLUE
* DEEP PINK PASTE COLOR

Tools

* ROLLING PIN
* BLOSSOM CUTTER AND VEINER SET
* 22 GAUGE FLORAL WIRE, CUT TO 4 IN (10 CM) IN LENGTH
* NOSE PLIERS
* CAKE DECORATING STAMENS
* CALYX CUTTER
* REJUVENATOR SPIRIT
* PAINTBRUSHES
* GREEN FLORAL TAPE

4 Pass the loose end of the wire through the center of the calyx shape. Use edible glue (see page 142) to secure it to the stamens. Paint the tips of the stamens with a deep pink paste color mixed with rejuvenator spirit. Leave it to dry.

5 Pass the loose end of the wire through the center of the blossom. Secure the flower around the calyx using edible glue. Hang upside down to dry.

6 Repeat steps 1–5 to make a few more cherry blossoms. Now attach them together in groups of 3. First, wrap green floral tape around each wire, starting from the top, just beneath the blossom, and working in a spiral along the length to the lose end of the wire. Now gather together 3 cherry blossoms in a bunch and use the floral tape to secure them together.

Orchid

Ingredients

* MODELING CHOCOLATE, COLORED WHITE
* EDIBLE GLUE
* PASTE COLORS OF YOUR CHOICE

Tools

* ORCHID CUTTERS AND VEINERS SET
* SCALPEL
* FOAM PAD
* BALL TOOL
* LARGE FLOWER FORMER
* PAINTBRUSHES
* 22 GAUGE FLORAL WIRE, CUT TO 4 IN (10 CM) IN LENGTH
* WHEEL CUTTER
* REJUVENATOR SPIRIT

1 Roll out some white modeling chocolate to a thickness of 1 mm. Cut out one piece using the orchid lip cutter.

2 Using a scalpel, cut the pointed extension of the orchid lip equally in half as shown in the picture here. Place them on a foam pad and use a ball tool to curl up the various parts of the orchid lips.

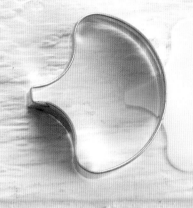

Look at pictures of different types of orchids to plan your color schemes, mixing flowers of different colors for a dramatic, impressive effect

3 Use the fan-shaped petal cutter to cut out 2 petals. Use the fan-shaped veiner to impress a pattern of veins on each of these petals.

4 Using the sepal cutter, cut one sepal shape. Use the sepal veiner to impress a pattern of veins on each of these petals.

5 Use a ball tool to soften the edges of all the sepal shapes.

7 Place the orchid lip into the center of the formed petals with the split petal pointing toward 6 o'clock and attach it with edible glue.

6 Place the sepal shape into the flower former with one petal pointing to 12 o'clock. Use edible glue to attach the 2 fan-shaped petals on either side of the sepal, one at 10 o'clock and the other at 2 o'clock.

8 Roll a small piece of modeling chocolate into a ball and pierce the tip of the length of floral wire into it. Secure the wire to the chocolate using edible glue. Use a wheel cutter to make an indent in the center of the ball. Pass the loose end of the wire through the center of the orchid and pull it through until the ball meets the flower. Secure the ball to the flower using edible glue. Let it dry for at least 24 hours. Once dry, use paste colors mixed with rejuvenator spirit to paint a design on the orchid.

Lantern

Ingredients
* MODELING CHOCOLATE, COLORED ORANGE
* EDIBLE GLUE

Tools
* WHEEL CUTTER
* ROLLING PIN
* SMALL CIRCLE CUTTER
* PAINTBRUSH

1 Roll a medium-sized piece of modeling chocolate into a ball. Flatten the ball slightly with your fingers to indicate the top and bottom of the lantern. Use a wheel cutter to make horizontal indents across the ball. Set aside.

2 Roll out some modeling chocolate to a thickness of 2 mm. Use a small circle cutter to cut out 2 circles.

Make a few lanterns, then insert fine floral wire through the loops at the top to suspend your floating lanterns over a cake

3 Glue one circle to one flattened side of the lantern. Glue the other circle to the flattened bottom. Roll a fine sausage of modeling chocolate and shape it into a handle. Use edible glue to attach the handle to the top of the lantern, using the picture here as a placement guide.

Fan

1 Roll out some modeling chocolate to a thickness of 1 mm. Cut out a large circle using a circle cutter. Cut the circle in half to create a semicircle. Use a small circle cutter to cut out a semicircle at the bottom of the fan.

2 To create the fan's ridges, place a toothpick beneath the shape so that it runs down the center of it and extends to the bottom of the fan. Now position more toothpicks beneath the shape at equal intervals, following the fan shape, until they approach the edges of the fan.

3 With the toothpicks in place, let it dry for 24 hours.

4 Remove the toothpicks, then paint a design on the fan using paste colors mixed with rejuvenator spirit. Leave it to dry. Roll some modeling chocolate into sausages of the same thickness as a toothpick. Position these at the back of the fan in the ridges molded by the toothpicks, and join them at the base into a fan handle. Use your fingers to blend the joins. Let it dry.

Ingredients

- MODELING CHOCOLATE, COLORED WHITE
- PASTE COLORS

Tools

- ROLLING PIN
- LARGE AND SMALL CIRCLE CUTTERS
- KNIFE
- TOOTHPICKS
- REJUVENATOR SPIRIT
- PAINTBRUSH

Ingredients

* MODELING CHOCOLATE, COLORED WHITE
* EDIBLE GLUE
* DARK GREEN PETAL DUST

Tools

* CUTTING WHEEL
* DUSTING BRUSH

1 Roll some modeling chocolate into thin sausages approximately 2–3 in (5–7.5 cm) in length. Using the cutting wheel, make deep indents along each length, spacing them roughly 1 in (2.5 cm) apart. Let it dry.

Bamboo

Use a leaf cutter to make leaves to apply to the bamboo stalks, dusting the leaves with a paler green dust color

2 Add some dark green dust color in each of the indents to create shadows. You can place leaves on the bamboo securing with edible glue (see *Leaves* on page 15).

Tea Set

1 To make the teapot body, roll modeling chocolate into a ball and push down gently on opposite sides to flatten. To make the lid, roll a smaller ball of modeling chocolate and push down to flatten. Use edible glue to attach the lid to a flattened surface on the pot body. Roll a tiny ball of modeling chocolate and glue this onto the center of the teapot lid. Let it dry.

2 Now make the spout. Roll some modeling chocolate into a small ball. Using your fingertips, tease the ball into a cone shape. Use a scalpel to cut the wider end at an angle to create the spout. Stick the spout to the side of the teapot with edible glue.

3 To make the teacups, roll some modeling chocolate into a small ball. Cut this in half with a scalpel and pull up the chocolate on each cut surface into the sides and rims of the teacups (or push a ball tool into the middle of a teacup and curl the edges up around the ball). Let it dry.

4 Make a small bamboo handle for the teapot (see page 90) and attach it to the body using edible blue. Paint a cherry blossom design onto the teapot and on the side of each teacup using paste color mixed with rejuvenator spirit.

Ingredients

* MODELING CHOCOLATE, COLORED WHITE
* EDIBLE GLUE
* PASTE COLOR OF YOUR CHOICE

Tools

* PAINTBRUSHES
* SCALPEL
* BALL TOOL (OPTIONAL)
* REJUVENATOR SPIRIT

Whimsical Woodland

Who can resist this adorable owl? Assemble a group of owls as toppers for a woodland-themed celebration cake.

Pom-poms

1 Roll out some modeling chocolate as thinly as possible. Cut out 6 shapes using a scalloped circle cutter.

2 Place a shape on the foam pad. Roll a ball tool around on the edges of the shape to curl the edges. Make sure the ball is half on the modeling chocolate and half on the foam pad, and use light pressure to avoid tearing the chocolate shape. Repeat with the remaining shapes.

3 Layer 5 of the shapes, using edible glue to secure each layer in the center. Place some scrunched-up tissue paper or plastic wrap between the layers at the edges. This helps to keep them separate and create a frill effect.

Ingredients

* MODELING CHOCOLATE, COLORED PALE PINK
* EDIBLE GLUE

Tools

* ROLLING PIN
* SCALLOPED CIRCLE CUTTER
* BALL TOOL
* FOAM DRYING PAD
* PAINTBRUSH
* TISSUE PAPER OR PLASTIC WRAP

4 For the last shape, fold it in half, then in half again, and secure this inside the center of the pom-pom using edible glue. Leave it to dry for 2 hours.

These half pom-poms look great on a cake or cupcake, but if you wish to suspend them over a cake, join two together, back-to-back, to create a rounded full pom-pom

5 Carefully remove the tissue paper from between the layers of the frilly pom-pom.

Hydrangeas

1 Roll out some modeling chocolate to a thickness of 1–2 mm. Cut out a flower using the hydrangea cutter.

2 Place the flower shape into the hydrangea veiner (you may need to dust the mold with cornstarch first if the veiner or modeling chocolate is sticky). Push down the hydrangea veiner, then remove the modeling chocolate from the mold. Place it on a foam drying tray to shape the flower. Leave it to dry.

Ingredients

- MODELING CHOCOLATE, COLORED WHITE
- GREEN AND PALE BLUE PETAL DUST

Tools

- ROLLING PIN
- HYDRANGEA CUTTER AND VEINER SET
- FOAM DRYING TRAY
- GREEN OR LILAC PETAL DUST
- DUSTING BRUSH

3 Once dry, give the center of the flower a dusting of green or lilac petal dust for a natural look.

Thread hydrangeas onto floral wire with a ball of white modeling chocolate attached to one end to make wired flowers

Mushrooms

1 Roll out some white modeling chocolate into a small ball, then roll this into a tapered length that's roughly 1 in (2.5 cm) long. Flatten the wider end into a base.

2 Insert a toothpick into the top of the mushroom stem, with the tip of the stick protruding from the top by ¼ in (5 mm). Leave it to dry.

3 Roll some dark pink modeling chocolate into a ball that's roughly 1 in (2.5 cm) wide. Push your finger into the middle to shape it into a semicircle. Alternatively, if you have one, use a half-ball mold to make this shape.

Ingredients

* MODELING CHOCOLATE, COLORED WHITE AND DARK PINK
* WHITE PETAL DUST

Tools

* TOOTHPICK
* HALF-BALL MOLD (OPTIONAL)
* REJUVENATOR SPIRIT
* PAINTBRUSH

4 Mix some white petal dust with rejuvenator spirit and use this to paint the white spots onto the mushroom cap.

5 Once the mushroom stem is dry, place the cap onto the toothpick protruding from the stem to secure it.

If you like you can dust the base of the mushroom's stem with brown petal dust to create the impression of dirt

Berries

1 Roll some dark red modeling chocolate into two balls. Slightly taper the end of one ball to mimic the distinctive strawberry shape. Taper one end of the other ball and flatten it on top to give it a raspberry shape.

Ingredients

* MODELING CHOCOLATE, COLORED DARK RED AND GREEN
* EDIBLE GLUE
* WHITE ROYAL ICING (OR WHITE NONPAREILS)
* CONFECTIONERS' GLAZE

Tools

* PAINTBRUSHES
* ROLLING PIN
* TOOTHPICK
* CALYX CUTTER
* PASTRY BAG
* SIZE 00 ROUND PIPING TIP

2 Roll out tiny balls of dark red modeling chocolate, then stick them onto the surface of the raspberry shape using edible glue. Flatten each of them once they are attached, and ensure there are no gaps in between them. Let them set.

3 Use the end of a paintbrush or a toothpick to make indents all over the strawberry. Roll out green modeling chocolate to a thickness of 1 mm. Use a rose calyx cutter to cut the strawberry leaf and secure to the top of the strawberry using edible glue.

4 Using the fine piping tip, pipe white royal icing into each of the indents on the strawberry to give the impression of seeds. Alternatively, push white nonpareils into each of the indents. Allow to set for 2 hours. Paint both berries with confectioners' glaze and leave them to dry for 20 minutes. Give the berries a second coat of confectioners' glaze and leave them to dry.

Insert green floral wire into the tops of the berries, then attach them in groups with large leaves made of modeling chocolate to make a berry plant

Fall Leaves

Ingredients

* MODELING CHOCOLATE, COLORED DARK YELLOW
* DEEP RED, GOLD, BROWN, OR ORANGE PETAL DUST
* TYLOSE POWDER

Tools

* ROLLING PIN
* MAPLE LEAF CUTTER AND VEINER
* DUSTING BRUSH
* FOAM DRYING TRAY

1 Knead some tylose powder into the modeling chocolate (see page 143). Roll out the modeling chocolate to a thickness of 2 mm. Use a maple leaf cutter to cut out the leaf shapes and add the pattern of the veins. Place the leaves over the ridges of a foam drying tray and leave them to dry.

2 Dust the maple leaves with petal dust with an autumnal color.

Flower arch

1 Roll modeling chocolate into 10 tiny balls. Dip the tip of a length of gauge wire into edible glue, then pierce a white ball with the coated tip. Push the other end of the wire into floral foam. Roll out modeling chocolate to a thickness of 1 mm. Use the miniature cutters to cut out flower and leaf shapes. Pierce the loose end of the prepared wire through the center of a flower and pull it through to bring the flower up to the ball. Use edible glue to secure the flower to the ball.

2 To create a leaf stem, pierce the end of a length of wire that has been dipped in edible glue into a leaf shape. Push the other end of the wire into floral foam and leave to dry. Then use petal dust colors of your choice to color the flowers and leaves.

3 Wrap some green floral tape around the wire to cover its length. Repeat with the remaining flowers and prepared wires.

Ingredients

* MODELING CHOCOLATE, COLORED WHITE
* DEEP RED, GOLD, BROWN, OR ORANGE PETAL DUST
* EDIBLE GLUE

Tools

* ROLLING PIN
* MINIATURE FLOWER AND LEAF CUTTERS
* FOAM DRYING TRAY
* DUSTING BRUSH
* 24 GAUGE FLORAL WIRE, CUT INTO 1½ IN (4 CM) LENGTHS
* FLORAL FOAM
* PAINTBRUSH
* GREEN FLORAL TAPE
* 18 GAUGE FLORAL WIRE
* WIRE CUTTERS

4 Curve a length of 18 gauge floral wire into an arch shape and trim it to your required size. Attach the flowers and leaves to the arch using the floral tape, starting with one flower at the top-center of the arch and working down one side, wrapping the tape around the wires of the flowers and leaves. Now work down the other side of the arch in the same way.

Acorns

1 Roll some pale brown modeling chocolate into a ball, then shape it into an oval.

2 Roll a tiny ball and flatten it into a cylinder shape. Use edible glue to attach this at one end of the oval to make the acorn stalk.

3 Roll out some dark brown modeling chocolate to a thickness of 1–2 mm. Use a small circle cutter to cut out a circle. Wrap the circle around the ball so that it extends halfway up its length, and attach it using edible glue (see page 142).

Ingredients

* MODELING CHOCOLATE, COLORED PALE BROWN AND DARK BROWN
* EDIBLE GLUE
* CONFECTIONERS' GLAZE

Tools

* PAINTBRUSHES
* ROLLING PIN
* SMALL CIRCULAR CUTTER
* SMALL TRIANGLE CUTTER

4 Use the corner of a triangle cutter to make indents in the brown modeling chocolate to mimic the texture of an acorn shell. Leave it to dry for 20 minutes.

5 Give the acorn, and not the dark brown shell, a coating of confectioners' glaze. Leave it to dry.

Owl

1 Roll some dark brown modeling chocolate into a large ball.

Ingredients

* MODELING CHOCOLATE, COLORED DARK BROWN, WHITE, BLACK, PINK, AND PALE BROWN
* EDIBLE GLUE

Tools

* ROLLING PIN
* SMALL CIRCLE CUTTERS IN 2 SIZES
* PAINTBRUSH
* SMALL ROUND PIPING TIP
* SMALL AND MEDIUM ROSE PETAL CUTTERS
* SMALL BLOSSOM CUTTER

2 Push down the top of the ball and pinch out both sides with your fingers to create the owl's ears. Flatten the body gently with the palm of your hand. Leave it to dry.

3 Roll out white modeling chocolate to a thickness of 1 mm. Use the larger circle cutter to cut out 2 circles for the eyes. Attach these using edible glue. Roll out black modeling chocolate to a thickness of 1 mm. Use the smaller circle cutter to cut out 2 circles for the pupils. Attach to the white circles using edible glue. Use a small round piping tip to cut 2 tiny circles from white modeling chocolate. Attach these to the pupils in the same way to give the eyes highlights.

4 Roll out some pale pink modeling chocolate to a thickness of 1 mm. Use the small rose petal cutter to cut out 6 petal shapes. Use edible glue to attach these to the owl's body in overlapping layers in a triangular shape, starting at the bottom of the owl. Offset the petals in each layer to create a scalloped effect.

5 Roll out some dark brown modeling chocolate to a thickness of 1 mm. Use the large rose petal cutter to cut out 2 petal shapes. Use edible glue to attach the petals to the sides of the owl to form the wings, using the picture below as a placement guide.

6 To make the nose, roll some light brown modeling chocolate into a small ball, then flatten the ball and pinch one side to form the beak. Attach this below the eyes using edible glue. Cut out a tiny blossom shape from the rolled out pink modeling chocolate using the small blossom cutter. Attach this to the base of an ear using edible glue. Leave it to dry.

Ranunculus

1 Roll some pale green modeling chocolate into a medium-sized ball. Using a star-shaped modeling tool, make a star-shaped indent in the center of the ball.

2 Using the circle cutters, make 2 circular indents of different sizes around the star shape using the smallest 2 circle cutters.

3 Roll out some pink modeling chocolate to a thickness of 1 mm. Using the third largest circle cutter, cut out 10 circles.

4 To attach the first layer of petals, position 5 circles around the green ball, overlapping each petal and securing them with edible glue. Make sure that the indented circles in the ball remain visible.

5 Attach 5 more circles in the same way to complete the next layer of petals.

6 Using the largest circle cutter, cut out 20 circles from the rolled out pink modeling chocolate. Attach these to the flower in the same way as before, ensuring you overlap the petals as you go. Place the flower in a flower former and leave it to dry.

Use a petal veiner to add veins to the flower petals if you would like them to have some texture

Ingredients

* **MODELING CHOCOLATE, COLORED PALE GREEN AND PALE PINK**
* **EDIBLE GLUE**

Tools

* **STAR TAPER CONE TOOL**
* **ROLLING PIN**
* **CIRCLE CUTTERS IN 4 SIZES**
* **PAINTBRUSH**
* **FLOWER FORMER**

Arabian Nights

Deep rich colors and antique gold are the focal points for this exotic theme. Learn how to make the most intricate designs using simple techniques.

Cushion

Ingredients

* MODELING CHOCOLATE, COLORED GREEN, BLUE, PINK, AND GOLD
* EDIBLE GLUE
* METALLIC GOLD EDIBLE PAINT

Tools

* ROLLING PIN
* RULER
* CRAFT KNIFE
* TOOTHPICK
* PAINTBRUSH

1 Roll out your modeling chocolate to a thickness of ½ in (1 cm). Using a ruler and craft knife (or a square cutter), cut out a 1¼ x 1¼ in (3 x 3 cm) square from each color.

2 Pinch out the corners of each square to elongate them.

Use a textured rolling pin or a textured mat to gently emboss a pattern into the cushion to emulate fabric

3 Flatten the edges of the squares all the way around the shapes.

4 Roll some gold modeling chocolate into one small ball, then roll this into a long, thin strip. Attach this around the edges of a cushion to suggest fabric trimming along the seams of the cushion. Repeat with the remaining cushions.

5 Use a toothpick to indent the gold edge you just attached to each cushion to give the impression of cord trimming. Then use gold metallic edible paint to paint swirls, hearts, and polka dots across the cushions.

Lamp

Ingredients

* MODELING CHOCOLATE, COLORED GOLD
* EDIBLE GLUE
* GOLD LUSTER DUST

Tools

* ROLLING PIN
* SMALL CIRCLE CUTTERS IN VARIOUS SIZES
* MINI SMILE TOOL
* PAINTBRUSH
* EGGCUP
* DUSTING BRUSH

1 Roll out some gold modeling chocolate into a medium-sized ball. Pinch out one side and elongate it into a long spout shape.

To make the lamp even more decorative attach some edible jewels or dragées for that extra bit of sparkle

2 To make a lid for the lamp, roll out some modeling chocolate to a thickness of 1 mm. Cut out a circle shape using a medium-sized circle cutter. Use a mini smile tool to indent a decorative pattern around the edge of the circle. Attach this to the top of the lamp using edible glue.

3 Roll a small ball of modeling chocolate. Use edible glue to stick this to center of the top of the lid to suggest a lid handle.

4 Roll a piece of gold chocolate into a long, thin sausage and shape into the handle. Leave it to dry. Attach the handle to the lamp using edible glue.

5 To make a base for the lamp, cut a circle using the larger circle cutter. Indent a decorative pattern in the circle using the smile tool and an assortment of small circle cutters.

6 Place the circle for the lamp base, with the patterned side facing down, into an eggcup to shape it. Leave it to dry for 2 hours. Once dry, attach to the bottom of the lamp using edible glue. Leave the assembled lamp to dry.

7 Give the lamp a covering of gold luster dust to finish.

Henna Stencil

Ingredients

* MODELING CHOCOLATE, COLORED PURPLE, GRAY, AND YELLOW
* SHORTENING
* GOLD LUSTER DUST

Tools

* ROLLING PIN
* HENNA STENCILS
* DUSTING BRUSH
* LARGE CIRCLE CUTTER

1 Roll out some purple, gray, and yellow modeling chocolate, each to a thickness of 1–2 mm. Place a stencil on top of each piece of rolled out chocolate and lightly roll over it with the rolling pin to encourage the stencil to stick to the modeling chocolate.

2 Using a fingertip rub a little shortening lightly over each stencil to expose the modeling chocolate through the holes in the stencil.

3 Using a dusting brush, dust gold luster dust over each stencil so that it sticks to the shortening.

4 Carefully remove each stencil, taking care not to smudge the design.

5 Use a circle cutter to neatly cut around each stenciled pattern. Leave it to dry on a flat surface.

Brooch

Ingredients

* MODELING CHOCOLATE, COLORED WHITE
* METALLIC PAINT OR LUSTER DUST

Tools

* BROOCH MOLD OR BROOCH AND FOOD-SAFE SILICONE PUTTY
* KNIFE
* PAINTBRUSH AND/OR DUSTING BRUSH

1 If you don't have a brooch mold, make one using a brooch. Prepare some food-safe silicone putty following the packet instructions and press the brooch into the putty. Let it to set for at least an hour, then remove the brooch.

2 Insert a ball of modeling chocolate into the mold. Trim away excess chocolate with a knife, then freeze for at least 15 minutes. Remove the chocolate from the mold. (It should slip out easily, but if it doesn't, return it to the freezer for a few minutes more.) Leave the molded chocolate on a flat surface to dry, then use metallic paints or luster dust to add detail to the brooch.

Tiles

Ingredients

* MODELING CHOCOLATE, COLORED PURPLE AND YELLOW
* EDIBLE GLUE

Tools

* ROLLING PIN
* DECORATIVE PAPER PUNCH WITH A SQUARE PATTERN
* CUTTING WHEEL
* PAINTBRUSH

1 Roll out some purple modeling chocolate to a thickness of 2 mm. Place the decorative paper punch on top of the chocolate and push down to create a decorative pattern. Punch out the pattern several times across the surface of the rolled out chocolate. Remove the punch and, using a cutting wheel, cut around 4 of the square patterns to enclose them in a border of unpunched chocolate. Set aside the offcuts from the punched designs to use in the next step.

2 Roll out the yellow modeling chocolate to a thickness of 2 mm. Using the cutting wheel, cut out squares that are roughly the same size as the punched squares. Arrange the purple swirls and angles onto each tile to make different designs, using edible glue to secure.

Love Birds

Adorn your cake with these sweet little love birds
—the perfect decorations on a cake for any nature
lover. Choose a soft color palette for a romantic
theme, or select bright colors for a cake for children.

Birds

Ingredients

* MODELING CHOCOLATE COLORED PALE GREEN, BROWN, PINK, AND WHITE
* EDIBLE GLUE
* BLACK EDIBLE PEN
* IVORY PEARL DRAGÉES

Tools

* ROLLING PIN
* 2 ½ IN (6 CM) CIRCLE CUTTER
* ROSE PETAL CUTTERS IN 4 SIZES
* PAINTBRUSH
* SMILE TOOL
* SCALPEL

1 Roll out some green modeling chocolate to a thickness of ½ in (1 cm). Use the circle cutter to cut out a circle shape.

2 Roll out some brown modeling chocolate to a thickness of 1 mm. Use the largest petal cutter to cut out a petal shape. Now use your fingers to bend the tip of the shape upward.

3 Roll out some pink modeling chocolate to a thickness of 1 mm. Use the second largest petal cutter to cut a petal shape. Now use the curve on the cutter to cut out a smaller piece for the bird's chest. Attach the chest to the bird's body with edible glue, using the picture opposite as a placement guide.

4 Use the third largest petal cutter to cut out a smaller petal shape from the rolled out pink chocolate for a wing. Make a pattern of indents with a smile tool to represent feathers. Attach the wing to the bird's body with edible glue, using the picture below as a placement guide.

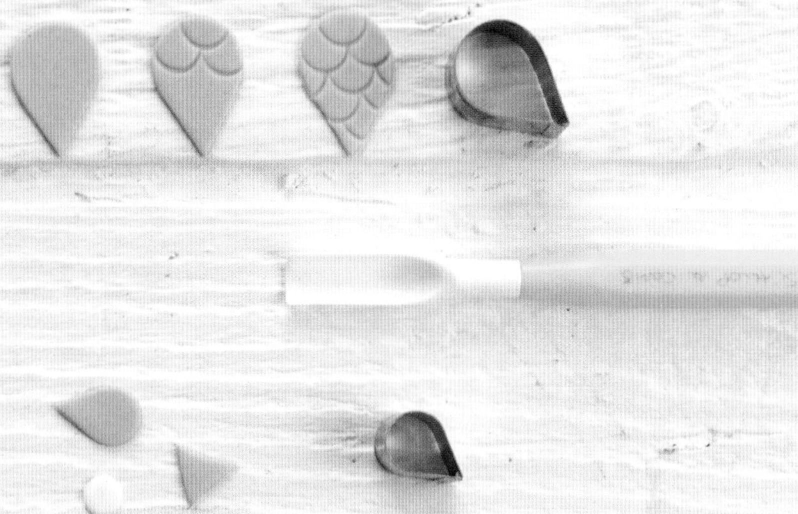

5 Use the smallest petal cutter to cut a petal shape, then trim off the tip to use for a beak. Attach this to the bird as shown in the picture below using edible glue. Roll out some white modeling chocolate to a thickness of 1 mm. Use a tiny circle cutter to cut a small circle for the eye. Attach this to the bird using edible glue, then complete the eye by drawing on a small black dot for a pupil using edible black pen.

6 Position the bird on the green circle and use edible glue to secure it. If you like, cut a flower shape from the rolled out pink chocolate using the tiny blossom cutter, and attach this to the bird's head as a decoration. Now draw the bird's legs onto the green circle beneath the body using black edible pen. Complete by attaching pearl dragées at regular intervals around the edge of the green circle with edible glue.

Birdhouse

Ingredients

* MARSHMALLOW SQUARES
* EDIBLE GLUE
* MODELING CHOCOLATE, COLORED GREEN AND PINK
* BLACK PASTE COLOR

Tools

* SHARP KITCHEN KNIFE
* PAINTBRUSHES
* ROLLING PIN
* CUTTING WHEEL
* WOOD GRAIN TEXTURE MAT
* SMILE TOOL
* SMALL CIRCLE CUTTER
* REJUVENATOR SPIRIT
* BIRDHOUSE PICTURE

1 For this project, you need to make a birdhouse shape using marshmallow squares, over which to apply the modeling chocolate. You may need 2 or 3 squares, depending on the size of the cakes you have. The internal birdhouse shape should be about 2½ in (6 cm) deep. Use a picture of a birdhouse as a guide to cut each square into a birdhouse shape. If you are using more than one square, align them—the squares are sticky, so they should stick together without the need for edible glue, if you push them together.

2 Roll out some green modeling chocolate to a thickness of 2 mm. Using a wheel cutter, cut around the roof panel template twice to make 2 roof panels.

3 Create a tile pattern on each roof panel by making indentations with a smile tool. Set aside.

4 Roll out some pink modeling chocolate to a thickness of 2–3 mm. Place the chocolate over the wood grain texture mat and roll over it with a rolling pin to indent the pattern into the chocolate.

5 Using a wheel cutter, cut around the birdhouse side panel template twice to cut 2 birdhouse side panels from the textured pink chocolate.

6 Cut out the front and back panels of the birdhouse in the same way, using the front/back panel template. Use a small circle cutter to cut a circle in one of these pieces for the entry hole.

This cute birdhouse can be created in a variety of colors to suit your theme. For a winter cake topper go for bolder colors, or chose red and gold for a Christmas theme

7 Using the cutting wheel, make vertical lines in the textured surfaces of the front, back, and side panels to give the appearance of wood panels.

8 Stick the front, back, and side panels to the marshmallow square structure using edible glue. Blend the joins with your finger. Attach the roof panels in the same way, blending the seam at the ridge of the roof with your finger. To complete the birdhouse, mix some black paste color with rejuvenator spirit and use this to paint any marshmallow square visible through the hole in the front panel of the birdhouse. Leave it to dry.

Birdcage

Ingredients

* MODELING CHOCOLATE,
  COLORED GRAY AND PINK
* EDIBLE GLUE
* WHITE ROYAL ICING

Tools

* ROLLING PIN
* KNIFE
* EGG CUP OR HALF-BALL
  MOLD WITH A 1¼ IN
  (3 CM) DIAMETER
* PAINTBRUSH
* PASTRY BAG
* FINE PIPING TIP
* SMALL BLOSSOM CUTTER

1 Roll some gray modeling chocolate into a large ball, then shape it into a thick sausage shape with a 1¼ in (3 cm) diameter. Trim the ends with a knife. Roll another ball of gray modeling chocolate and push it into the egg cup or half-ball mold to give it a domed shape. Leave it to dry.

2 Align the dome shape with one end of the sausage shape to make the birdcage shape. Join them together using edible glue—don't worry if the seam is not neat as it will be covered.

3 Using royal icing in a pastry bag, pipe horizontal and vertical lines around the shape, covering the seam to suggest the bars of the cage. Roll out pink modeling chocolate to a thickness of 1 mm. Cut out some blossom shapes using the small blossom cutter. Using edible glue, attach these to the birdcage at various points to finish.

Bird's Nest

1 Roll out some brown modeling chocolate to a thickness of 2 mm. Using a cutting wheel, cut out a number of thin strips and trim them to approximately 1-in (2.5-cm) lengths. Make the sizes irregular to give the nest a natural look.

2 Layer the pieces randomly in a hexagonal pattern to resemble a bird's nest. Secure the pieces to one another using edible glue.

Ingredients

* MODELING CHOCOLATE, COLORED BROWN AND WHITE
* EDIBLE GLUE

Tools

* ROLLING PIN
* CUTTING WHEEL
* PAINTBRUSH

If you have a sugar gun, use the grass disc to create long, thin strips of brown modeling chocolate to use as twigs for a different effect

3 Roll some white modeling chocolate into 3 small balls, then roll them into ovals. Place these in the middle of the nest, securing them with edible glue.

Teddy Bear Picnic

Sunny the Hedgehog and her best friend Zoe the
Bunny are enjoying their homemade picnic while Luke
the Bear, who's eaten too many sandwiches, has fallen
asleep! Let your inner child run wild to bring your own
stories to life.

Teddy Bear

2 To make the arms, roll some dark brown modeling chocolate into 2 small tapered sausage shapes. Flatten the wider ends, ensuring they have the same circumference as that of the smaller circle cutter. Roll out some pale brown modeling chocolate to a thickness of 1 mm. Cut out 2 circles using a small circle cutter. Use the small piping tip to indent 3 circles at 1 edge of each circle to resemble paws. Use edible glue to attach the paws to the ends of the arms. Attach the arms to the sides of the body piece with edible glue, using the picture opposite as a placement guide.

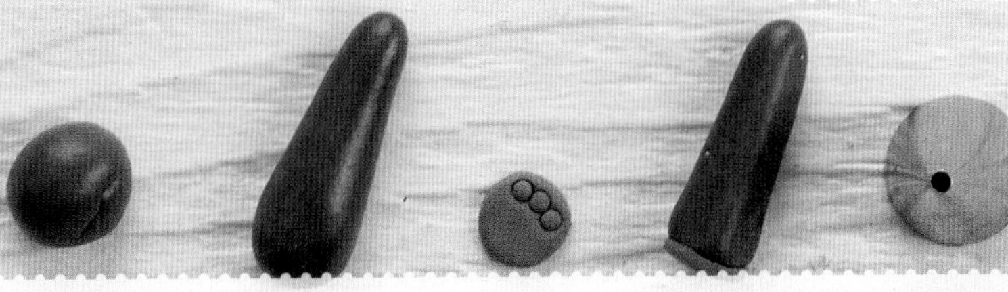

1 Roll some dark brown modeling chocolate into 2 balls—a large ball for the body, and another that is two-thirds the size of the first ball for the head. Set aside.

3 To make the legs, roll dark brown modeling chocolate into 2 tapered sausage shapes. Pinch and flatten the wider ends to create feet, ensuring they have the same circumference as the larger circle cutter. Use the circle cutter to cut 2 circles from the rolled out pale brown chocolate. Use the larger piping tip to indent 3 circles at 1 edge of each circle to resemble paws. Use edible glue to attach the paws to the feet and the legs to the sides of the body piece.

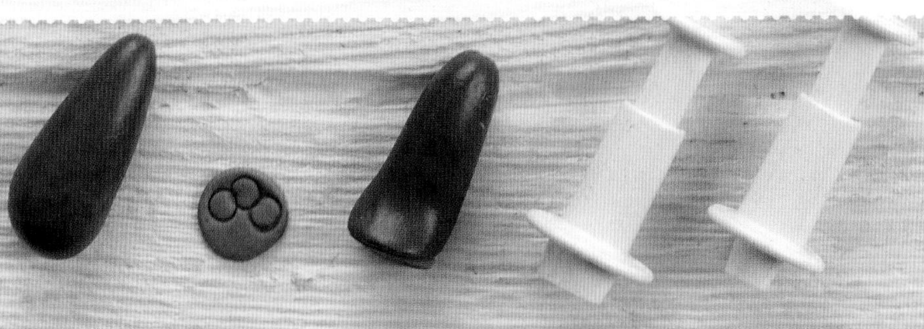

4 For the ears, roll out dark modeling chocolate and cut out a circle using the larger circle cutter. Cut a smaller circle from the pale brown chocolate. Stick the smaller circle onto the larger one using edible glue. Cut the circle in half. Pinch together the straight edge of each half and attach to the head.

5 To make the muzzle, roll some pale brown modeling chocolate into a small ball, then flatten this with your finger into a slightly oval shape. Use a toothpick to make an indent in the center for the mouth and use a wheel cutter to make a line from the mouth to the edge of the oval shape.

6 Attach the muzzle to the head using edible glue. Roll 2 small balls of black modeling chocolate for eyes, and a slightly larger ball for the nose. Attach the nose to the muzzle, and the eyes to the head, using the picture here as a placement guide. Attach the head to the body, then use the toothpick to suggest the bear's navel. Leave it to dry.

For a girl bear, add a bow at the top of the head, then draw on long, curly eyelashes using a black edible pen

Ingredients

* MODELING CHOCOLATE, COLORED DARK BROWN, PALE BROWN, AND BLACK
* EDIBLE GLUE

Tools

* ROLLING PIN
* SMALL CIRCLE CUTTERS IN 2 SIZES
* SMALL PIPING TIPS IN 2 SIZES
* PAINTBRUSH
* WHEEL CUTTER
* TOOTHPICK

Bunny

1 Roll some yellow modeling chocolate into a medium-sized ball for the body and another ball half the size of the body for the head. Place the larger ball into the large petal cutter to give it a teardrop shape, then flatten it gently with the palm of your hand.

2 Roll out white modeling chocolate to a thickness of 1 mm, then cut out another teardrop shape with the smaller petal cutter. Stick this onto the body with edible glue (see page 142) to make the tummy.

3 For the ears, roll some yellow modeling chocolate into 2 small balls, then roll them into tapered sausages. Use the end of a paintbrush handle to make an indentation in each ear to suggest a crease. Flatten one end of each ear to make a base. Set aside.

4 Roll some white modeling chocolate into 2 small balls, then use your fingers to tease them into teardrop shapes. Flatten the shapes with a finger. Use a cutting wheel make 2 little indents to suggest the paws. Attach the paws to sides of bunny with edible glue, using the picture opposite as a placement guide. Repeat this process with slightly larger balls of white chocolate to make the feet.

5 For the muzzle, roll a medium-sized ball of white modeling chocolate into an oval shape and flatten it with a finger. Use a smile tool to indent a smile on the muzzle. Use a cutting wheel to indent a line from the smile to the edge of the oval to represent the nose crease. Stick the muzzle onto the head with edible glue, using the picture here as a placement guide. Now stick the ears into the correct positions in the same way.

6 Roll a tiny ball of pink modeling chocolate, shape it into a tear drop for the nose and stick this into position on the muzzle. Using a black edible marker, draw on the eyes. Now stick the head to the body using edible glue.

To add whiskers, insert small mock flower stamens on either side of the bunny's nose

Ingredients

* MODELING CHOCOLATE, COLORED YELLOW, WHITE, AND PINK
* EDIBLE GLUE
* BLACK EDIBLE MARKER

Tools

* PETAL CUTTERS IN 2 SIZES
* ROLLING PIN
* PAINTBRUSH
* WHEEL CUTTER
* SMILE TOOL

Hedgehog

Ingredients

* MODELING CHOCOLATE, COLORED DARK BROWN AND BLACK
* EDIBLE GLUE

Tools

* BALL TOOL
* SMALL STAR PIPING TIP
* PAINTBRUSH

1 Roll brown modeling chocolate into a medium-sized ball.

2 Pinch out one end of the ball to form the snout.

3 Using the small end of the ball tool, make 2 indents for the eyes just above the snout.

4 Using a star-shaped piping tip, make indents all over the body of the hedgehog to suggest spines.

5 Roll some black modeling paste into 2 tiny balls and 1 slightly larger ball.

Try piping on brown royal icing using a grass piping tip for an alternative way of creating the hedgehog's spines

6 Insert the 2 tiny balls into the eye indents. Attach the larger ball at the end of the snout nose.

Ladybug

Ingredients

- ❋ MODELING CHOCOLATE, COLORED RED, BLACK, AND WHITE
- ❋ EDIBLE GLUE
- ❋ BLACK EDIBLE MARKER

Tools

- ❋ CRAFT KNIFE
- ❋ CUTTING WHEEL
- ❋ TINY CIRCLE CUTTER

1 Roll some red modeling chocolate into a medium-sized ball. Cut it in half with a craft knife. Place the cut side on your work surface and shape the modeling chocolate into an oval using your hands.

2 Use a cutting wheel to indent a line along the length of the center of the oval. Use a black edible marker to draw on the ladybug's spots.

3 Roll some black modeling chocolate into a small ball. Cut this in half. Use edible glue (see page 142) to attach the flat side to one end of the ladybug to make the face.

4 Roll out some white modeling chocolate to a thickness of 1 mm. Use a circle cutter to cut out 2 tiny circles for the eyes. Attach these to the face using edible glue. Draw a black dot onto each eye with black edible marker to suggest pupils.

Insert mock flower stamens into the head on either side to give the ladybug antennae. First, cut them in half and paint them with black edible paint

Picnic foods

Ingredients

* MODELING CHOCOLATE, COLORED WHITE, PINK, GREEN, AND RED
* EDIBLE GLUE

Tools

* ROLLING PIN
* CIRCLE CUTTER
* PAINTBRUSH
* SQUARE CUTTER
* CRAFT KNIFE

1 Roll out each color of modeling chocolate to a thickness of 2 mm. For the cake, use a circle cutter to cut out 3 white and 2 pink circles. Now align them in a stack, starting and finishing with a white circle, and use edible glue to stick them together. Roll some red modeling chocolate into tiny balls and arrange these on the top of the stack, as shown in the picture below, to represent cherries. Use a craft knife to cut a small slice from the cake, ensuring the slice has a cherry on it.

2 To make the sandwiches, cut squares—2 white, 1 green, and 1 red. Align these in a stack, starting with a white square, followed by green, then red, then white again. Stick them together using edible glue (see page 142). Use a craft knife to the stack into 4 equal squares, then cut each of these into triangles.

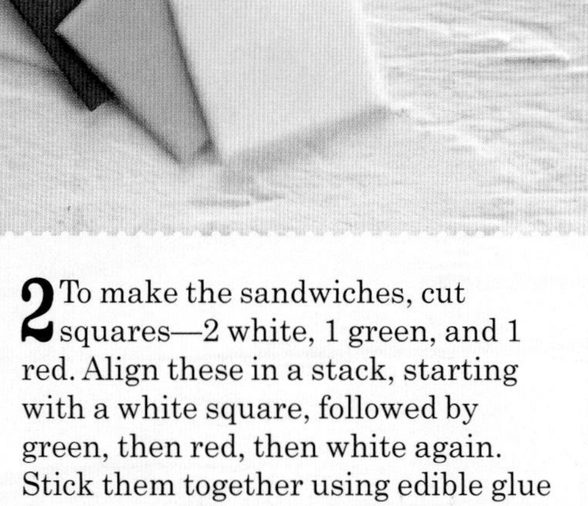

Picnic blanket

1 Roll out both the pink and gray modeling chocolate to a thickness of 2 mm. Using the square cutter, cut out 13 squares of each color.

2 Arrange the squares in a check pattern of 5 x 5 squares. Lightly roll a rolling pin over the top to merge the squares together, taking care not to distort the shape too much.

Ingredients

* MODELING CHOCOLATE, COLORED GRAY AND PINK

Tools

* ROLLING PIN
* SQUARE CUTTER

Tips & techniques

Creating beautiful cake toppers using modeling chocolate is easy when you know how! The following tips will help you on your way to creating stunning cake decorations for every occasion.

Softening petal edges

Softening the edges of your floral cake toppers will help to make them look more realistic.

1 Place the petal onto a foam pad.

2 Place your ball tool right on the edge of the petal so it is positioned half on the petal and half on the pad. Soften the petal by gently applying pressure around the edge of the petal.

3 Run the ball tool around the circumference of the petal—this movement will soften the petal.

Curling petals

For some of the projects in this book, the petals are curled upwards. To achieve this you need to use a foam pad and a ball tool, but the movement is slightly different to the Softening Petal Edges technique above.

1 Place the petal onto a foam pad.

2 Place your ball tool at the tip of the petal and gently apply pressure. Gently move the ball tool toward the middle of the flower.

3 Release when you get to the middle, and the petal will have curled up.

Making edible glue

Edible glue can be purchased ready-made; however it's also very easy to make. You can use royal icing to stick heavier decorations to cakes, but edible glue is thinner and has the advantage of being invisible when dry.

1 Place ¼ teaspoon tylose or CMC powder into a small container with a lid. Add 1¼ tablespoons of cooled boiled water, secure the lid and shake well.

2 Leave the glue to rest and thicken overnight.

Adding tylose powder

Tylose powder is an edible firming agent. Use ¼ teaspoon of the powder for every 3½ oz modeling chocolate. Make a well in the chocolate and add the tylose. Knead well, then wrap in plastic wrap and leave for about 2 hours. Re-knead before use.

Using floral wire

Inserting a topper into floral wire gives the illusion that the topper is suspended—perfect for creating a showstopping centerpiece. In accordance with food safety guidelines in some countries, you may be advised not to insert the wire directly into a cake. If this is the case, you will first need to use a flower pick made from food-safe plastic to provide a barrier between the wire and the cake.

1 Cut the floral wire to the desired length and dip the end in edible glue.

2 Insert the wire into the topper and leave it to set. Once set, the wire can be inserted into the cake.

Using gum paste

Gum paste can be used instead of tylose powder to achieve a more elastic, firmer modeling chocolate that can be rolled out very thinly. Mix modeling chocolate with gum paste using a 50:50 ratio.

Mixing edible paint

Edible paints are available from most good cake decorating suppliers; however mixing your own using dust or paste colors will enable you to achieve the desired shade and consistency.

1 In a paint palette, mix together your paste or petal dust of choice with a few drops of rejuvenator spirit until it is thick but still runny.

2 To lighten the color, add in some white or super white powder (this is great for mixing up pastel shades).

Index